D0519940

bubblefacts...

PLUNDERING PIRATES

miles KELLY

PUBLISHING

First published in 2005 by
Miles Kelly Publishing Ltd
Bardfield Centre, Great Bardfield, Essex, CM7 4SL

Copyright © Miles Kelly Publishing Ltd 2005

2 4 6 8 10 9 7 5 3 1

Publishing Director:
Anne Marshall

Senior Editor:
Belinda Gallagher

Editorial Assistant:
Hannah Todd

Designer:
Louisa Leitao

Cartoons:
Mark Davis

Production:
Estela Boulton

All rights reserved. No part of this publication may be stored in a retrieval system, or transmitted by any means, electronic, mechanical, photocopying, recording, or otherwise, without the prior permission of the copyright holder.

ISBN 1–84236–536–3

Printed in China

Library of Congress Cataloging–in–Publication Data
is on file at the Library of Congress.

Indexer: Jane Parker

www.mileskelly.net
info@mileskelly.net

Contents

Terror from the sea
pirate attack

A pirate is a robber on the ocean. Pirates attack ships and ports, stealing treasure and other goods. The Greek islands were home to some of the earliest pirates. Around 500BC, there were many ships trading along the Mediterranean coasts. They were easy prey for the pirates.

BY HOOK OR BY CROOK!

IT'S RUDE TO POINT!

HA HA! YOUR TREASURE OR YOUR LIFE!

MORE STUFF FOR THE YARD SALE!

Early pirates stole amber, copper, and silver and stashed it away on their island hideouts.

In 67BC, the Roman leader Pompey wanted to stop pirates stealing Rome's food supplies.

Viking invaders raided the British coast. Even Julius Caesar was captured by pirates—but then released.

Caught by corsairs

kidnapped!

Pirates of the Mediterranean were known as "corsairs." They hunted people, not treasure. Corsairs sold ordinary captives as slaves or forced them to work in their galleys. Richer people were more valuable. The two most feared corsairs were the Barbarossa brothers. They lived during the 16th century.

Galley slaves were forced to row the big heavy oars. They were chained together at the ankle.

In 1816, a fleet of English and Dutch ships attacked a group of corsairs near Algiers on the North African coast. The corsairs were forced to release over 3,000 slaves.

The Barbarossa brothers were so-called because of their beards. Barbarossa means "Redbeard" in Latin.

Some slaves tried to escape by land, while others risked the dangers at sea. Very few got away.

Trail of treasure across the ocean

From the early 1500s, Spanish galleons carried vast amounts of treasure across the Atlantic. Loaded with American gold, silver, jewels, and other riches, these big vessels were heavily armed. But they were also slow and heavy, and attracted pirates like bees to a honeypot.

Francis le Clerc was a fierce pirate who had a wooden leg. He captured Havana in Cuba and set it alight.

Soldiers guarding the Spanish treasure were called "conquistadors." They were the first of the Spanish soldiers to invade South America. Conquistadors often traveled with the treasure ships, but were no real match for the pirates.

Spanish galleons sailed in groups to protect themselves from pirate attack.

Wily sea dogs serving the Queen

John Hawkins made many raids on treasure ships in the Spanish Main. However, he didn't call himself a pirate. He carried a letter from Queen Elizabeth I of England, which allowed him to attack ships from an enemy nation. Hawkins, and many like him, were called "privateers."

Hawkin's letter allowed him to attack any ship—he became very rich.

Francis Drake was the greatest of the Elizabethan "sea dogs." He first went to sea at 14, and later joined his cousin John Hawkins on his expeditions. Like Hawkins, he became a privateer, and carried on an unofficial war against Spain.

can you believe it?

Drake risked death by raiding a treasure store but when the store was opened, it was empty!

In 1572, Drake ambushed a mule train laden with treasure, which he gave to the Queen.

Most pirate ships had to be small and fast. On the Spanish Main, many were "schooners," with two masts. The captain's cabin was in the stern (back), while the crew slept in the middle of the ship. Treasure, gunpowder, and food were kept in the hold.

Below deck it was cramped, smelly, and noisy. Pirates barely had room to put up their hammocks.

Most pirates dressed like other sailors of the time. They wore short blue jackets, checked shirts and baggy canvas pants. However, some showed off the finery they had stolen, such as velvet pants, black felt hats, silk shirts, and crimson waistcoats with gold buttons and lace.

In calm weather, there was little for the pirates to do. They would mend ropes and sails, or gamble with dice. In bad weather, or when they were chasing another ship, life was very busy. The crew might have to climb aloft in the rigging to alter the sails, keep lookout from high on the mainmast, or prepare the cannon for firing.

Fresh food was hard to obtain onboard a ship, so the cook served dry cookies and pickled meat.

Storms
at sea
shipwreck

A pirate's biggest nightmare was shipwreck. Violent storms could spring up suddenly, especially in the warm seas of the Caribbean. In 1712, a hurricane brought racing winds and giant waves into Port Royal harbor in Jamaica, smashing 38 ships.

Sometimes ships were blown and carried toward treacherous rocky shores when a storm sprung up.

Storms could drive helpless ships onto a rocky shore. In 1717 the pirate ship *Whydah* was heading for Cape Cod, off North America, loaded with booty. A storm pushed the vessel onto rocks. The mainmast fell down, and the *Whydah* started to break up. Only two of the crew reached land alive.

There were few ways to cope with an emergency. If the ship was leaking, sailors could try pumping out the water. If the ship ran aground, they could throw heavy objects overboard, such as cannon or food barrels. This made the ship lighter, and ride higher in the water.

WHEEE!

EYE SPY WITH MY LITTLE EYE...

CHEST THE TRICK!

SPLASH!

rates found their way across the ocean with skill and luck, and with the help of a compass and a sextant.

Grace O'Malley commanded a pirate fleet on Ireland's west coast. She went to sea as a young girl, and later moved into a stone castle on the coast. Her fleet of sailing ships attacked passing vessels. In 1593, Grace begged Queen Elizabeth for a pardon. She lived to be over 70 years old.

Anne Bonny and Mary Read were braver than their male crew, who hid rather than fight the British!

can you believe it?

Grace o'Malley cut her hair short to look like her sailors. They all nicknamed her baldy!

One of the greatest women pirates was Ching Shih. When her husband died in 1807, she took over his raiding fleet on the Chinese coast. She was a brilliant leader and forced her sailors to obey a strict set of rules.

NEVER UNDERESTIMATE A WOMAN!

I'LL HAVE NOODLES, FRIED RICE...

YEAH YEAH!

BANG!

Ching Shih was said to feed her captives on just caterpillars and rice.

Hunting the pirates
navy power

European countries started to build bigger and stronger navies. With these, they were able to begin ridding the sea of pirates. Well-armed navy fleets patrolled the trouble spots. Pirates were offered free pardons if they gave up their lives of crime.

Edward Teach was the most terrifying pirate on the oceans. He was better known as Blackbeard.

Large rewards were given to anyone who helped to capture pirate ships, but it was a dangerous task.

Blackbeard made himself look as frightening as possible by plaiting ribbons in his beard and putting lighted matches under his hat. One man was not afraid of Blackbeard—naval officer Robert Maynard.

In 1718, Maynard cornered Blackbeard. He leapt aboard his ship and fought him to the death.

When a pirate captain decided to attack, he raised a special flag. Not every pirate flag was the famous skull-and-crossbones. Most early pirates used a bright red flag to frighten their victims. Black flags became popular in the early 1700s, with pirates adding their own symbols.

Once aboard, the pirates would have a bloody fight—often the merchants would simply surrender.

Merchants often hid their cargo. The pirates had to search everywhere and tear apart walls and doors to find it. They might even torture their captives until they told them where it was hidden.

Bartholomew Roberts was probably the most successful pirate ever. He never drank anything stronger than tea!

JUST THOUGHT I'D **DROP** IN!

I'LL STAY UP HERE, THANKS.

I'M A BAREFOOT BANDIT!

I'D RATHER WALK THE PLANK!

Pirates threw ropes with hooks on the end at the enemies' sails, and used them to climb aboard.

Pirate plunder

pieces of eight

All pirates dreamed of gold and silver. Some were lucky enough to capture ships packed with silver coins, gold bars, or finely made ornaments. However, most merchant ships carried humbler goods, such as cloth, coal, or iron.

The captain shared the loot among his crew. He did this very carefully so that no one complained.

Pirates also needed everyday things. If they had been away from land for several weeks, they would be glad to steal food, drink, and other provisions. Fresh guns, cannon balls, and gunpowder always came in useful!

Can you believe it?

one of the most valuable cargoes of all was spices from India and Sri Lanka!

SO, HOW MUCH DO **YOU** THINK YOU'RE WORTH?

WELL, I'M WORTH MORE THAN HIM!

POLLY... LOTS OF LOLLY!

SQUAWK!

BLING!

BLING!

Pirates would hold a rich person captive, and demand a ransom. "Pieces of eight" were used as currency.

Buried treasure

x marks the spot

Pirates hid their treasure by burying it in a remote spot.

Many believe that William Kidd buried a vast store before he was captured. His piracy had gained him a huge amount of cargo, most of which he sold or gave to his crew. When he was arrested in 1699, Kidd claimed he had hidden $187,000 (£100,000) of treasure.

FINDERS KEEPERS!

HERE WE GO AGAIN!

SIGH!

NO, WE'RE **NOT** BUILDING SAND CASTLES!

Hmmm, I'M NOT GOOD WITH MAPS...

Pirates drew maps of where they buried their treasure so that they would be able to find it again.

After attacking a mule train, Francis Drake found that his ships had sailed away. He ordered his men to bury the loot. Then he made a raft, paddled out to find his ships, and brought them back. Drake then dug up the treasure and put it onboard.

There was no code of conduct between pirates, so they would steal treasure from each other, too.

Desert islands
marooned!

Some pirate captains had strict rules. "Black Bart" Roberts made his crew promise to keep to a code of conduct. They could not gamble or fight onboard ship, or keep lights and candles burning after 8 o'clock at night. Anyone who brought a woman on board, or who deserted the ship, would be put to death or marooned.

The Pacific islands were mainly uninhabited, so castaways used their wits to survive.

Marooning was a terrible fate. The pirate was left alone on a deserted island while his friends sailed away. He was given a few vital things but it was almost impossible to escape, and food was hard to find.

Can you believe it?

Alexander Selkirk was stranded on a desert island off the coast of Chile in 1704. He survived there for five years!

SOB! BUT I MISS MY MOM!

SHARKS THINK THEY OWN THE PLACE!

Sometimes pirates would even maroon their captain! Many castaways did not survive for long.

Crime and... punishment

Many captured pirates were shipped back to Britain in chains. But most never got that far. They were taken to the nearest American port and executed as quickly as possible. Only the younger criminals were pardoned and released.

Before and after trial, the pirates were kept in prisons that were foul, smelly, and overcrowded.

Judges were keen to condemn pirates as quickly as possible, so that any still at large would be scared.

Pirates that were found guilty were hanged. As a warning to others, their bodies were put on display.

Pirate characters
book, movie, play

The best-known pirate of all is in a story—Long John Silver. With the one-legged villain (Silver), crazy castaway (Ben Gunn) and lots of buried treasure, Robert Louis Stevenson's *Treasure Island* has thrilled countless readers since it first appeared in 1883.

Long John Silver is famous for his pet parrot and wooden leg. Captain Hook is Peter Pan's arch enemy.

Many of us get our ideas of pirates from watching movies. Ever since cinema began, pirate movies have been popular. These movies usually show a fun-filled picture of pirate life, and leave out most of the savagery.

The story of the dreaded Blackbeard was actually put on stage in 1798 as a ballet!

The Pirates of Penzance is an operetta about pirates who are too kind to steal from orphans!

Index